THE

SECRET *TO* FINANCIAL HEALTH *FOR* WOMEN

THE

SECRET *TO*
FINANCIAL
HEALTH *FOR*
WOMEN

Everything Your Mother Never
Told You About Creating Wealth

DEBORAH A. NILES, MD, FAAFP

THE SECRET TO FINANCIAL HEALTH FOR WOMEN
Copyright © 2021 Deborah A. Niles
All rights reserved.

Published by Publish Your Gift®
An imprint of Purposely Created Publishing Group, LLC

Printed in the United States of America

ISBN: 978-1-64484-508-0 (print)
ISBN: 978-1-64484-509-7 (ebook)

Special discounts are available on bulk quantity purchases by book clubs, associations and special interest groups. For details email: sales@publishyourgift.com or call (888) 949-6228.
For information log on to www.PublishYourGift.com

Dedication

I dedicate this book to the loving memory of my parents, Veronica Rosaline Niles and Ronald Toney Niles. My mother's love, dedication, and passion are what first brought us to the United States. She left her life behind in London, England, to move to the United States in order to fulfill her duty as a nurse and fill the nursing shortage at the time. My father and my siblings followed her and immigrated to Brooklyn, New York, three months later.

My mother worked tirelessly as a nurse and would come home weary but still made sure that she took care of me and my siblings. She encouraged me to be a physician when she saw my deep love of people and wanting to nurture and take care of them. She didn't have a 529 educational savings plan or whole life insurance saved up for my college years, but she did have some bonds that she cashed out when there was a need. She helped me throughout my college and medical school years. She even helped me as a resident when my student loan debts became a burden and felt overwhelming. She helped me when I went to buy my first house. She gave me $3,000 cash and said to put it in my checking account because you can't go and apply for a mortgage without money in your account. I can go on and on about the wisdom that my mother has shared with me. She was right about so many things. Like all mothers, they usually know best.

My father was the true rock and backbone of our family. When I think of him, he is the reason that I love sports and cars so much. My father worked all of his life and then retired and was diagnosed with cancer shortly after he retired. He lived two more years, and I will always treasure the time that I spent with him. My father loved sports, and he spent a lot of his free time in front of the television. So, I learned early on that if I was going to get some time with him, I would have to sit with him and watch whatever he was watching. I watched baseball, football, basketball, boxing, and even NASCAR races. My friends are puzzled, especially about my love of cars and car racing. It really traces back to the time and the conversations that I had with my dad while watching television. As a result, yes, I am a daddy's girl and all the trim that goes with it. My father never put pressure on me to go into any specific field. He just wanted me to get an education and be successful and good at whatever I chose.

I also dedicate this book to the loving memory of my older sister, Felicia Elizabeth Niles, who was also known as Lizzie. She was fierce, persistent, bold, and loving all at the same time. She was also a nurse like my mother and a lot of my aunts and cousins. She made us walk through places that I wouldn't ordinarily walk through. She would stand up for herself and for me if she had to in school. There was no way anyone was going to bully me because once they learned who my sister was, they would shrink and go back to their little corner. I watched her fight three of the toughest girls in elementary school, and all I could think about was how that was a fair fight. She held her own and didn't need my help. That was the type of woman and sister that she was. I will forever be grateful to her and the lasting memories she has left me with. We talked almost every day, and although I miss our talks, she lives on in my heart, and I will forever be grateful to God for making her part of my family.

I would also like to thank my brother, Lawrence Niles, for being the best brother ever and for all of the encouragement that he provided for me during this book writing process. My brother is one and a half years younger than me. We have a great relationship and talk as often as we can. The most memorable thoughts of him are from the many family vacations that we have had together since childhood. I would like to thank you for joining me on these family vacations and adventures. We have memories and pictures to last a lifetime. I would also like to encourage you to write all of the books that we have talked about over the years. Your audience is waiting for you.

To all of my nieces and nephews, I say thank you. Jordan Dorsey, your creativity has given me the spark and courage to write this book. Vaughn Dorsey, your thoughtful and caring ways mean a lot to me. You call just to talk and to check up on me. I love that about you. Andre Niles, although we don't talk often, you are always in my heart and prayers. I love your creative spirit and the wonderful artist that you have become. Trevor Niles, you bring love and consistency to the

Niles family. Keep being true to yourself. Warren Niles, I love your fortitude and strength. Keep being the best version of yourself that you can be. Ashley Niles, you are the youngest of the tribe, and in so many ways, your warm spirit is like the gift that keeps giving.

I dedicate this book to my friends, cousins, and the rest of my family with the last names Duff, Parris, Vaughn, Callender, Branche, Chichester, Williams, Dorsey, and too many others to name. Our family spans the globe from Africa, Asia, Europe, South America, the Caribbean, and Canada to the United States of America. I want to thank you for being part of my family. All of you have touched my life in so many ways.

I want to thank and dedicate this book to my friend Dr. Joyleen Earle, a cardiologist in Pennsylvania and New York. She has challenged me to look at other areas of investing such as options trading and cryptocurrency. She has shown me that you can invest in other investment vehicles and meet your long-term investment goals at the same time.

I want to thank and dedicate this book to my friend Dr. Susan Lashley, a maternal fetal medicine specialist in Morristown, New Jersey. Whenever we talk, she reminds me of the money talks that we had as residents in our separate residency programs. I was training in family medicine, and she was training in obstetrics and gynecology. Our paths crossed when I rotated through the Obstetrics Department where she was training. As I was writing this book, she reminded me of all of the things that she learned from me about credit, buying a house, getting a mortgage, buying a car, investing, and saving for retirement. She said that I also taught her the importance of reading your employee benefit package and the value that is in it.

I dedicate this book to my classmates at Bronx High School of Science, University of Pennsylvania, Drexel University College of Medicine, and UMDNJ-Robert Wood Johnson Medical School Department of Family Medicine Residency Program. I also dedicate this book to my sorors in the Epsilon Phi Chapter and Philadelphia Alumnae Chapter of Delta Sigma Theta Sorority, Inc.

I would also like to thank my business coach, Dr. Drai, and the Medical Moguls Academy for allowing me to be a part of the Academy. It is through his hard work and dedication that I learned the skills that are needed to run a business. Thank you for your time and patience. I am eternally grateful, and I appreciate you! To Publish Your Gift for making this book experience possible.

Table of Contents

Foreword

My name is Dr. Loretta Long, EdD. I am an actress, singer, motivational speaker, video producer, educator, and author. I have a doctorate in education and I played Susan on the famous children's show *Sesame Street* for over fifty years.

Dr. Deborah and I met in church about eighteen years ago in New Jersey. I am so glad that she has written this book, *The Secret to Financial Health for Women*. This book is much needed today. I know that the information that she has at her fingertips can make such a difference in all people's lives, not only women's.

She helped me implement a plan on budgeting, paying off debt, and raising my credit score. She has shown me how you can turn your savings into long-term investments. She also helped me face financial issues that I didn't want to face. You cannot fix what you aren't willing to confront. In her compassionate way, she will help you to face your financial issues. She has a way of simplifying things so you can understand and implement them.

In her soothing, mommy-like voice, she will give you the courage to face any difficult financial decision that you will have to make. I am so happy that she wrote this book. This book will improve so many people's lives. I hope you enjoy this book as much as I have.

Dr. Loretta Long, EdD

Preface

My name is Dr. Deborah Niles, and I am board certified in family medicine. I have practiced in my specialty for over twenty years, and I have seen the impact that finances have on people's health and lives. As a family physician, you learn that you have to care for the whole patient and not just the one or two things that bring them into the office. We have to address the physical health, mental health, and financial health of our patients.

Money can be one of the biggest stressors on an individual's or family's life. It is important to address all of these areas especially when the need arises. I learned that there was no point of prescribing a medication that the patient didn't have money to pay for or wasn't reasonably covered by their insurance.

Health insurance should be made available to all and at a reasonable cost if people are going to sign up for it. As a society, we have moved toward this effort with the Affordable Care Act, which is the comprehensive healthcare reform law that was enacted in March 2010. This act is also known as the ACA, PPACA, and Obamacare.

When I was in medical school, I started to incur a lot of student loan debt, and it continued to grow until it had almost doubled in size because of the high interest rates that were attached to these loans. Once I started residency and started earning a salary, some of these student loans could no longer be deferred, so I had to start paying them back.

I had to quickly learn what a budget was and how to create one and stick to it. As women, most of us don't get these money talks from our mothers, because in some instances, our fathers may have handled the finances in our families or our mothers weren't taught by their mothers or fathers.

In these pages, I'm going to teach you the secrets of what credit is, how to create an effective budget, and how to accumulate wealth by saving, investing, and paying your debts off. I'm also going to show you how you can create generational wealth so you can leave a legacy to your children and grandchildren. You are going to learn the same secrets that I have shared with my closest family members and friends. You, too, can be a millionaire in your lifetime and have that money transfer to your children and grandchildren. This isn't a get rich quick scheme. This plan involves careful planning with your financial planner, time, patience, and consistency of saving and long-term investing. This is all possible, especially if you start at a young age and do this over time.

Introduction

The purpose for my writing of *The Secret to Financial Health for Women* was to introduce or re-introduce some basic money strategies and tips for saving and investing while managing your household on a budget. I thought it was important to do this, especially during these times that we are living in where the COVID-19 pandemic has altered so many of our lives and livelihoods.

Some of us have had to pivot because of lost wages or elimination of our positions.

So many of our households are run by women. Some of them may or may not have had the money talk from their parents. Unless we take a course or enroll in a degree program in the financial sector, most of us won't know basic money and budgeting tips because they aren't taught in school.

Let's face it. Most of us learn about money from watching our parents and their attitude toward money. Others learn from the media or observing or talking to their friends. You now are holding in your hands an excellent way to learn the financial tips and secrets that I will be sharing with you. Even if you learn just one thing from this book and apply it to your life, it can be life-changing down the road.

In this book, we will cover an array of topics that should get you well on your way toward wealth accumulation and generational wealth. We will cover in this book: financial planning, saving and budgeting, employee or fringe benefits, credit, retirement, estate planning, debt management, investments, taxes, and creating generational wealth. I recommend that you take notes, highlight, and refer back to the different chapters as needed.

Financial Planning

MONEY MINDSET

Having a good money mindset is important in financial planning. Money mindset is your attitude toward money. It is the leading driver in how you make financial decisions. Having a good and healthy attitude toward money will usually lead to good financial decisions. As a result, it can affect how you plan and achieve your goals.

Having a positive mindset usually causes you to be focused and decisive when it comes to planning and making money decisions. If you think and visualize yourself making a decision about your finances, you are more likely to make a decision and to take action. In contrast, negative thoughts lead to negative emotions and feelings, which can cause you to feel defeated or fearful. Either emotion will eventually lead you to not taking action on a financial decision that you need to make.

Moving from poverty and scarcity requires changing your mindset or attitude toward money. It takes time and practice to do this. Having abundant thoughts and prosperous thinking requires daily work in your thought life. Instead of focusing on what you don't have, start focusing on what you do have and develop an attitude of gratitude.

Gratitude is an emotion or feeling of appreciation that can be expressed or received. It has been studied and shown in Harvard Health Publishing that expressing gratitude can make you happier. People who are grateful tend to feel better, move better, sleep better, and heal better. It can also open the door to more relationships, since people generally want to be around positive-thinking people. People who practice gratitude daily also find that journaling their gratitude reinforces their feelings of gratitude. It can become a nice reference of the things that have happened to you for which you are grateful when you are dealing with a negative emotion or feeling.

In summary, having a healthy money mindset will help you develop good planning and spending habits that will last you a lifetime. By thinking good and positive thoughts, you will start to feel good and then express those positive thoughts to the world. Being grateful and thankful will strengthen your mindset. Journaling will help you remember the things for which you are grateful, and it will continue to fuel a positive outlook on money and life.

GETTING A PROFESSIONAL VS. GOING SOLO

Most people hire a professional to help them construct a comprehensive financial plan that they can utilize. There are many benefits to hiring a professional, including the fact that they have experience and training in the area of expertise that you are seeking. They can help guide you and save you the time that it would take for you to do all of your financial planning.

A certified financial advisor can create a financial plan which includes investment, estate, tax, and retirement planning. These types of plans are very comprehensive and can take hours to construct. I would recommend doing your research and checking the credentials of anyone you plan to hire. I would also recommend looking for references and customer ratings before you hire someone. The best financial advice that I got was from the financial advisor I hired and paid. Your financial advisor invests time into you, and they want to do a great job so you can give them a high rating and they can in return get more customers. Sometimes we tend to value the things that we have to pay for. I certainly do and I am still using that advice on a daily basis.

FINANCIAL GOALS

It is important to set a goal or target date for where you want to be or aim for it in the future. This goal usually involves your earnings, savings, investing, and spending. Your earnings over time can add up to a substantial amount of money. The money that you save from your earnings can impact the quality of your retirement years. Investing some of your earnings will help you achieve your financial goals, especially if you consistently invest with a long-term strategy in mind.

How much you spend over time can also impact the amount of money that you have in retirement.

Setting up a target goal for your future and retirement will help you stay focused on your daily tasks and remind you of what you are doing. It is the consistency of earning, saving, and investing balanced with spending that will help you achieve your goals. Initially it can feel like a lot to manage, but over time, it gets easier to do.

So what is that target date for retirement? It can be any age at which you feel like you will achieve that goal. Most people choose their target date or age at which they plan to retire based on the government program of Social Security. Social Security sets target ages of sixty-two, sixty-seven, or seventy and determines an estimation of your monthly benefit payments based on your thirty-five years of highest earned income. In other words, if you worked for forty of your sixty-seven years, then the highest thirty-five years become part of that formula that determines your monthly benefit payment that Social Security will pay you.

CREATING A ROADMAP FOR YOUR MONEY

The first step in creating a roadmap for your money starts with getting a financial planner. They can give you direction and help you get clarity on your goals. You have to define your goals and then set them. You have to decide if you want to create generational wealth and leave a legacy to your children and for generations to come.

Once you get a financial planner, you need to roadmap a plan that includes evaluating your C.R.E.D.I.T. C stands for credit. R stands for retirement. E stands for estate. D stands for debt. I stands for investment. T stands for taxes. This comprehensive plan will get you on your way to wealth accumulation and generational wealth. I will cover these topics in depth in later chapters.

In your plan, you have to look at all sources of income, including full-time, part-time and side gig income. Having multiple streams of income is a great strategy for accumulating wealth. Finding something that you are passionate about is another way to generate money doing something that you love.

The next step is getting a savings strategy. It is recommended that you save at least 10 percent of your income. You should save at least three months, preferably six months, in emergency funds. These funds will pay and cover your expenses during unforeseen changes, such as job loss or severe illness.

If you are an employee or business owner, this is the time to look at those fringe benefits, such as company matches for retirement savings, tuition benefits, mobile phone discount plans, and home and automobile purchase discounts. If you are part of any national, state, or local memberships, this is the time to check and see if they have any discount savings programs that can save you hundreds to thousands of dollars when you make an automobile purchase.

Giving back and donating can be a nice way to contribute to society and help for the greater good. A tithe, one tenth of your earnings, can go to charity if you choose to. Some people give what they are comfortable giving.

In addition to a written plan, creating a vision board that maps your goals out in picture form allows you to look at a visual picture of your goals. You can clip pictures or phrases that represent your dream and goals and pin them to your vision board. I find this very helpful. It is also a great reminder of the goals toward which you are working.

ACHIEVING YOUR FINANCIAL GOALS

Achieving your financial goals requires a financial plan and planner. The financial planner and you will determine how often you need to meet in order to review the financial plan. You also need a contingency plan if life events happen that will change your goals. If you lose your job or become ill or disabled, achieving your goals will be affected.

CHAPTER 2

Saving and Budgeting

SETTING UP YOUR ACCOUNTS

The first thing that you need to do is to decide which type of bank account you want. You will need to discuss with your financial planner the types of accounts that you need to open. The types of accounts that are available at your local bank will be personal checking and savings. If you own a business, you will be able to open business checking and savings accounts.

As an employee, you will have access to a financial services corporation or a brokerage firm to invest money toward your retirement. As a business owner, you will also be able to invest money into one of these corporations or firms. The government sets limits on the amount you can save pre-tax or after taxes.

One of the best investment products that is available if your modified adjusted gross income (MAGI) is under the government maximum is a Roth IRA (Investment Retirement Account). You can save a maximum amount of money that is set by the government depending on your age tax free. A Roth IRA offers you tax-free growth and tax-free withdrawals in retirement. You have to keep your account open for at least five years and be at least fifty-nine and a half to withdraw money tax free without a 10 percent penalty.

PAY YOURSELF FIRST AND BE CONSISTENT

As your income increases, you should remember that the percentage of money that you save can increase from 10 percent to the percentage that you chose as a goal. Paying yourself first is the most important thing that you can do with your savings. It places the value on the most important person—you. Without you and your savings and investments, there will be no wealth creation or generational wealth.

You can automate weekly, biweekly, or monthly transfers of your earned income through transfers or direct deposits into your savings or checking account. Self-automaton and consistency of saving a predetermined amount of money will get you to your financial goal faster. Doing this same behavior year after year will allow your money to grow exponentially over time.

Exercising consistency means that you continue to save and invest even though it may seem like your goal is out of reach at times. Each month and year of saving and investing brings you closer to your goal. One day you will wake up, and you will be at your destination. You will know that you are there because the goal amount of money that you planned to have in retirement or at a defined point in time outside of retirement will be there sitting in your account.

At least once a year, you should reevaluate your financial goals with your financial planner. Take a look at what you are saving and investing to see if you are on track. Any salary or life changes could also be a great time to reevaluate your goals.

It is recommended that you set a schedule to log into your accounts and check your deposits and balances. It is important to remember that if you have short and/or long-term goals to stick to that plan. Your investment balances can go up and down, especially with market shifts, but it is important to rethink and reevaluate your financial goals and only make changes if necessary.

DEFINITION OF A BUDGET

A budget is a detailed financial plan for the money that you earn or have over a defined period of time. That period of time is usually a year. Creating a budget allows you to look at the money that you earn on a monthly basis and allocate it to spending, savings, investments, and debts. This will allow you to track every dollar that you earn and how it gets allocated to the different areas mentioned above.

Knowing where your money is going gives you the control that you need over your finances. It allows you to plan for when you are ready to buy a house, car, or any large-ticket item. It also prepares you for life changes or unpredictable events such as illness. It also will help you prepare for the home or car repairs that you will encounter if you own, rent, or lease these items.

Budgeting is a necessity and gives you control over your finances. It allows you to look at what you earn and have in a realistic fashion. One of the things that helped me was to create a budget and test it. I would look at my budget every month and try to refine it. I would look for areas where I could spend less money so I could allocate more money to my savings, investments, or debts. These month-to-month budget analyses can really impact your finances over time.

Creating a budget and sticking to it will help you achieve your goals of wealth accumulation and ultimately creating generational wealth. Achieving and accumulating wealth takes planning, diligence, consistency, and action. You have to put in the work to create a plan that will allow you to manage your household efficiently. Knowing where every dollar that you earn goes is so important to staying on budget. Remember that creating a budget is part of the master plan of wealth accumulation and creating generational wealth.

CREATING A BUDGET

Most people recommend using the 50/30/20 rule when you create a budget. It means allocating 50 percent of your income or money to your needs, 30 percent to your wants, and 20 percent to your savings and debts. I recommend to further divide the 20 percent into at least 10 percent to savings and 10 percent to debts. You can adjust the numbers to fit your comprehensive financial plan.

The first step in creating a budget is to look at your net income or take-home pay. Your net income is the amount of money that you deposit weekly, biweekly, or monthly into your personal savings or checking account. Most people know their annual gross income. If you divide that income into twelve months, then you will get your monthly gross income. Your net income is the amount of money that you have left after your deductions are taken out of your paycheck. Your net income is what gets factored into your monthly spending. I would put this number on the top of your monthly budget sheet.

The second step is to list your monthly expenses or spending according to the 50/30/20 rule. I recommend starting with your needs, which is about half or 50 percent of your budget, then looking at your wants, which is usually about 30 percent of your budget. It is important to distinguish between what is a need and what is a want when you are creating a budget. You need a place to live, so that is a need, whether you decide to buy a home or rent an apartment. You may prefer to buy a car and drive to work because it is convenient, but public transportation may be more affordable than buying and maintaining a car. Remember that cars require maintenance and insurance, which are additional expenses.

The third step is to create a list of your expenses. I would recommend starting with your largest expense which is usually your home mortgage or apartment rental. The next item that I would recommend listing is your form of transportation, such as car loan, car lease payment, or train or bus expenses. The next thing I recommend including on the list is the amount spent on groceries, fast food, restaurants, and coffee. The next item should be expenses for clothing, uniforms, dry cleaning, and laundry. Don't forget to include the amount you spend on your personal appearance, like haircuts, manicures, and pedicures. Lastly, don't forget to include entertainment and vacations. As you can see, the list of expenses can get very long and can vary from month to month. That is why it is so important to look at your budget every month, because it will change.

It is really important to track your spending, and there are many ways you can do this. Your bank or credit card companies can itemize your spending into different categories such as auto, home, food, and travel. You can also use financial or accounting software to assist with tracking. If you prefer to hire someone to assist you, you can hire a bookkeeper and CPA (Certified Public Accountant), especially if you are self-employed.

SPENDING AND STAYING ON BUDGET

Tracking your spending and staying on budget takes daily, weekly, and monthly management. You have to plan for the unforeseen events that can occur, such as an illness or job loss, and you have to be ready to make a quick decision. Every purchase or payment that you make has to go through the budget plan and has to be scrutinized if you are going to stay on budget. This is key to staying on the budget that you created. One poor decision could cost you to have a deficit in your budget and can set you back temporarily.

My approach to spending and saving is to ask myself, "Is this a need or a want? Can it wait until another time?" Wants can always be deferred until another time. A need has to be looked at in real time. I ask, "Is this something that I need right now, and if not, how long can I defer this?" For example, your washer breaks down and you estimate that it will take either $250 to repair it or $250 to $2,000 to replace it. In the meantime, you have to wash your clothes, and while you wait on your decision to repair or replace your washer, you can go to the nearest laundromat and wash your clothes. Now you have to decide if replacing the washer is a need and whether to put it in the 50 percent column or a want and thus to put it in the 30 percent column.

UNDERSTANDING YOUR SPENDING HABITS

Learning how to adjust your spending habits is very important to maintaining and sticking to a budget that you create. If you know that you have a need that has come up and you have to include it in this month's current budget, you will have to decide which thing that you want can be deferred until a later date and time. This is one way that you can stay within your monthly budget.

It is important to understand what your spending triggers are. If overspending is tied to your emotions, that will have to be an area that you work on in order to curb your spending. It is important to have a healthy money mindset and not let your emotions take over and cause overspending. Meditating, journaling, and expressing gratitude are important and healthy habits to have that will help curb your spending. Staying laser focused on your financial plan goals will help you get through the difficult times in your life.

Other factors that affect your spending are your mood, energy level, peer pressure, and lifestyle. People tend to impulse shop when they are upset, stressed, or have low energy levels. If you are out shopping with a friend and they buy something, you may feel pressured to make a purchase also. It takes a lot of discipline to shop with a friend and not buy anything. Lastly, being accustomed to a certain lifestyle can be difficult to adjust from when hardship strikes. In summary, we have to constantly monitor our spending triggers and make the necessary adjustments if we want to stick to our budget and comprehensive financial plan.

When it comes to the 20 percent of your budget that is generally allotted for savings and debt, I try to adhere to the 20 percent rule and allot at least 10 percent to savings and 10 percent to debt. Your savings, which can include your investments, will mature over time and will be key to how you live in retirement and how much you can leave to your legacy.

Because I had a lot of medical school student loan debt, I made paying off my debts like working a part-time job. I became laser focused on maximizing my savings and investments while I was paying my debts down. I knew that reducing my debts would free up more money for saving and investing. I will review the strategy that I used to pay down my debts in a later chapter called Debt Management.

GENERAL BUDGETING TIPS

The most effective and efficient way to wealth creation is formulating a comprehensive plan. Creating a budget and sticking to it is the best budgeting strategy. You have to take out the time to create a budget and maintain it. Keeping it simple and understandable is also important. You have to be able to go back and look at your budget plan and see where it can be improved. This is a constant thing you have to do regularly if your budget is going to be effective and sustainable.

One big recommendation that most advisors give is to use cash for our purchases so you won't build up credit card debt. This is a sure-fire way to get your debts paid off while keeping your credit card balances low to zero. Keeping your credit card debt below 20 to 30 percent of your credit card limit is a great way to maximize your credit score. For example, let's say your credit card limit on Credit Card A is $1,000 and your balance is $200. If you have another credit card and need to make a purchase and you don't have available cash, use another card that has no revolving balance on it if possible so you won't impact your credit score that month.

There is a direct correlation between your debt to credit limit ratio. For example, I paid off one of my credit cards and watched my FICO credit score go up 30 points in one month. FICO score is what most banks use for mortgages and car loans. We will cover FICO and credit scores in more detail in a later chapter. I would recommend this strategy if you have a big purchase coming up within the next year, such as buying a house or a car, and you will need to borrow money to pay for it from a bank. Banks generally don't like to see large purchases too close together, so if you need to purchase a house and a car, purchase the house first.

One strategy that I used to create more available cash for saving and investing was to use credit cards that offered a reward system such as points for my spending. I would then use the points instead of cash to purchase other items, such as airline tickets or hotel stays. I would apply this system to the 30 percent want budget area. I recommend this strategy if you are disciplined and plan to pay your credit card balances in full at the end of the month. For example, if you have accumulated 50,000 points on one of your credit cards over time and the cash value of those points is equivalent to $500, you can use the points for your next purchase and save the $500 in your account. You now have an extra $500 in your account that can go toward savings, investments, or paying your debts down.

The travel industry's point system can be very valuable and rewarding when you use it as cash. Airlines, hotels, and most stores have created a point system that translates into cash, as I mentioned above. They sweeten the deal with additional bonus points if you sign up for their credit card. You have to decide if you sign up for these systems, whether it is better to pay with cash or use points for the purchase.

Other ways that you can generate points in some of your point system accounts is by paying your phone or utility bills with one of your credit cards that offers points for spending. Some cards can offer up to five points per dollar spent. You can easily generate points at the end of the year to make a purchase with points instead of using cash. You can save the cash and use the cash toward the 20 percent of your budget that is allocated to paying down your debts if you have any left or investing it toward your retirement savings. I would only recommend using this system if your credit card doesn't charge a 2 to 3 percent fee for paying your bills with the card.

Another well-kept secret that I discovered when booking a hotel reservation for travel was that it can be cheaper to book two reservations and have the hotel combine them into one when you arrive. For example, when you book a five-day stay, one of those days, such as a Wednesday, may have a higher daily rate than the other days. Sometimes it is cheaper to add an extra day or book two separate back-to-back reservations. For example, if you are traveling from Wednesday to Sunday for a conference or vacation, it may be cheaper to arrive the evening before your event and book a Tuesday through Friday stay and then a Friday through Sunday stay and then merge the reservations upon arrival. I recommend checking all scenarios because our ultimate goal is to save dollars so you have more for savings and investing.

Airlines have a lot of mystery built into their flight prices, but there is a method to their seemingly complex system. One travel tip that I learned and that I am happy to share is booking a mid-week flight on less-traveled days such as Tuesday and Wednesday. I recommend booking as early in the day as possible because the flight prices go up throughout the day as those initial early morning bargain fares are sold. For example, the airlines now share how many seats they have available at the price you are currently looking at when you are booking your flight. I know because I tested this by waiting, and then when I went to purchase the flight, it was available at a higher price.

Booking your flights after midnight on Tuesday morning if you are still up can get you the best prices. I was up late one Monday evening booking travel and thought that I was getting a great deal. Less than fifteen minutes later, it was midnight, and that same flight that I booked dropped by a few hundred dollars. You bet that I stayed up rebooking that flight because it was a long-haul flight. I saved several hundred dollars, which now can go toward savings and investments. We will talk more later as to why this is important and how it can impact your long-term savings and investment goals.

The next area of budgeting tips that can save you a lot of money over time is gas purchases. Gas prices, like airline prices, tend to fluctuate throughout the week and tend to be higher on weekends and holidays and during summer months. Gas prices also tend to be higher when the gas station is near or on a major highway. I know this because I observed this over time. Technology has made it very easy to track gas prices at the various gas stations. All you need is a phone and to download a gas app. This tip can translate into hundreds of dollars in savings a year and will give you more money to save or invest.

Coupon clipping is an old and effective way to rack up savings in your budget plan. This is an old method that I watched my mother use, and she could really stretch a dollar. Most supermarkets, pharmacies, and warehouses now have clipless coupons or an app that you can download and add coupons to your account. I generally check these while I am waiting in line or if I remember before I enter the store. Again, all of these savings translate into extra money for saving and investing.

Another coupon strategy is to look at the offers that your bank and credit card companies have on their apps or website. Each month they put out new offers that may or may not benefit you. It requires you to log in to their website and manually add these offers, which are like coupons. It could be a percentage or dollar amount off from a specific company. For example, you may get an offer for a pharmacy at which you already shop for $5 off your next $5 spend over the next thirty days. You were planning to go there anyway to purchase a necessity.

You go and add on the offer, and it automatically comes off of your bill when you check out and make your purchases.

Some of this may seem tedious or time consuming, but your goal is to save at least $1 or more a day over a long period of time with compounded interest so you can get the benefit of accumulating wealth to enjoy in retirement and pass along a legacy to generations to come. Balancing your budget requires time, patience, re-evaluation, and discipline. You should use every opportunity to save money when you can. Every $1 saved and reinvested will grow and make your future brighter and more prosperous.

If you are an active-duty military officer, there are numerous benefits available, such as a percentage off of your purchases, special mortgage and car loan rates, and waived airline baggage fees. Cell phone providers sometimes offer special discounts to active-duty and retired military personnel and their families. Some banks have created special divisions to assist active-duty military.

Due to the COVID-19 pandemic, healthcare workers can now enjoy reduced rates at hotels and other establishments. These special rates can be booked through their app or website using a special designated code. It never hurts to ask if there are any available benefits when you are making purchases. All of this will increase your available savings.

One of the biggest budgeting tips that will save you a lot of money is to decrease or eliminate your cable or television service. I know this is a sore spot for most people, but cable and television services have increased tremendously over the years. I remember when cable bills were as low as $19.99 a month. Today, I have seen cable, television and other packages cost as much as $199 a month or more depending on if you get some of the movie and sports packages.

I ask myself, "Why do we spend so much on entertainment when there are so many free options out there?" If we took $100, for example, and applied that to an investment strategy that we will talk more about later, that could yield a large sum of money in retirement. If we took the $99, for example, and applied it toward our debts, we could be debt free or close to it when we reach retirement. These money-saving strategies can be applied to our budgeting, and they can make our lives a lot easier in the long run.

Getting rid of my cable bill was one of the best decisions I could have made nine years ago. My cable bill started out at about $30 a month, and then it grew to about $90 a month. That is $360 a year to $1,080 a year. I saved $12,960 over the nine years by getting rid of my cable service. At first it felt strange, not having cable, but I got used to it. Most of the time when I wanted to sit and watch a movie, I realized that there was nothing that I wanted to watch, or I had already seen it.

I was able to apply the $90 a month that I saved by not paying for cable toward investing in my retirement through my employer's 403(b) plan and paying my debts down. In summary, any time you can reduce or eliminate an expense and apply that money to that 20 percent of your budget that includes savings and paying your debts, that is a win-win situation for you. This may seem like a small amount of money, but when you think about how $1 a day or $30 a month invested at an interest rate of 10 percent over fifty-six years can grow to $1,000,000, it will change how you look at $1 moving forward. Yes, saving $1 a day or $30 a month could yield you $1,000,000 growing at 10 percent compounded interest over fifty-six years. Just imagine the $90-a-month cable bill going toward your investments growing at 10 percent compounded interest over fifty-six years turning into a whopping $3,000,000.

I used the cable bill as an example, but there are many other examples that could be used. You can look at that 30 percent of your budget that is comprised of your wants. If you are buying coffee drinks for $2 to $5, five days a week, just scaling back your purchases in that one area could leave you with more money for the savings and debt section of your budget. It could be your love of clothes, shoes, or bags. There could be splurges in other areas in your life. I'm not talking about clothing as a necessity in the 50 percent of your budget where you have your needs. I'm talking about having clothing, shoes, and bags but wanting more.

If you are willing to wait and buy some of those items you want later in the season or off season, you may be able to get them at a discounted price. You can also shop at discount stores or consignment stores. You can get some of the best deals at some of these places.

It is so important that you get this. This was me and is a lot of people. We spend money on things that are depreciating assets and that will ultimately not add value to our lives. One large-ticket item that most of us have purchased many times in our lifetime is a car. The minute you sign the paperwork, buy that car, and drive it off the lot, it has depreciated. Most cars depreciate about 20 to 30 percent in the first year and then depreciate another 15 percent a year for up to ten years. After ten years, your car is worth about 10 percent of what you paid for it. Just think that if we purchased that car pre-owned for one to two years, we would save about 35 percent or more for a two-year-old car. Cars are built to last longer today than they were thirty to forty years ago, so this is a good strategy to use.

If the price for a new car is $25,000 and a pre-owned one- or two-year-old car is $20,000 or less, the $5,000 that you save could be put toward building your emergency savings account, retirement investments, or paying your debts off. Purchasing your car at the end of the month or the end of the season before next year's model comes out is another savings tip. You can save additional money by using these two tips.

Some auto manufacturers offer a membership for which you sign up at least one year prior to buying the car. As a member, you can get additional savings off of the car you are purchasing. Checking your other memberships to see if they partner with that car manufacturer can save you additional money through discounts. All of this can add up to thousands of dollars in savings off of your next auto purchase.

When the auto dealerships offer you money for the car you just purchased, you say no until you pay that car off. The purpose is to get you to buy a newer model and to keep you locked into a new depreciating asset that they call a new car with new payments. The car payments may be $10 or $20 less than you are currently paying, but now you are locked into a longer car payment. For example, you took out a five-year car payment loan at $500 a month. You have paid off three years of car payments, and now they offer you a new car at $475 for another five years. You are still left with five years of payments on a newer model instead of the two years of payments left on your current model. That new car that you just bought now becomes a used car when you drive it off the lot.

The cars that are being built today are more durable than cars of the past. You can buy a car today, pay it off, and keep that car if you choose for another five or ten years. If you service that car, wash it, and keep it clean, it should easily last you five to ten years or more. By not buying a car every three to five years, you will be saving at least $25,000 that you could put toward investing in your future or paying your debts down. This will help get you on your path toward debt freedom, wealth accumulation, and generational wealth.

These budgeting tips and tactics really can affect your finances over time. Now just imagine if you could apply this same strategy to other areas of spending, how much more money you could have in retirement. Just imagine being able to take any vacation you wanted or to live in a house that was paid for. Just imagine driving a car that was paid for because you set up a budget and actually stuck to it over the years. This strategy can help you achieve wealth and debt freedom, build generational wealth, and allow you to leave a legacy to your children and grandchildren.

CHAPTER 3

Employee or Fringe Benefits

OVERVIEW

Your employee benefits can help contribute to your savings. Normally when you start a new job, you get an orientation from human resources on your benefits. It is critical that you attend this session or read your employee benefit package. Most of this information is now available online, so you can read it at your leisure.

I would advise you to spend the time reading through every benefit that is listed. Be sure to read the qualifications for each benefit carefully. I would also advise that you read it at least twice in case you miss something the first time. I would carefully look at the registration dates and deadlines and check the website for updates on policy changes regularly. Sometimes employers add new benefits for which you may only get communication through an email, letter, or the website.

Most employers offer group life insurance, disability insurance, and long-term care insurance policies. Most of these policies typically end when you end your employment with that company. Some of these policies may be portable, so I would find out which policies are portable and what the premiums would be when you end your employment. Knowing and understanding your employee benefits, especially the portable plans, can be beneficial to you and translate into hundreds to thousands of dollars in savings. The reason this is important is because group policies tend to be cheaper than individual policies. It could cost you a lot more money to get the same plan on your own if that plan isn't portable.

TIME OFF

Paid time off (PTO), sick days, vacation days, and federal holidays are usually some of the biggest perks that an employer offers. PTO is paid time off or personal time off that an employer grants you with pay. Some employers pool these days, and others separate them. Once you figure out how your time is allotted to you, it is important to track your time so you know what is available. Although it is rare that errors are made in electronic systems, you still need to look at your time and check it to see if it matches your personal time log. The error can come in when the data is entered into the system.

You also need to know how many days you are entitled to and how much notice you need to give before you request any type of time off. You are more likely to get an approval of the time off request when it is made in advance. The same applies to sick days with the exception of when you are ill. You need to know how your sick time can be used and the protocol for notifying your supervisor or employer.

Lastly, but equally important, you need to know if you can accrue or carry over PTO and sick and vacation days into the next year. You also need to know if your employer uses a calendar year, which is usually from January to December, or an academic year, which is usually from July to June. Know the calendar that your employer uses and stick to it.

In summary, it is critical that you track your time. Nothing is worse than finding out on June 30 that your academic year is ending and that you have unused PTO or vacation days that you can't carry over into the next year. I have seen this happen to several people, so I urge you to track your time and use it.

INSURANCE AND DISABILITY BENEFITS

One of the most coveted and expensive employee benefits is health insurance. I would spend ample time reading the difference between the different health insurance options if they are offered. When finances are tight and you don't have the luxury of picking the best plan, most people will go with the cheapest payroll deduction in this category. I would encourage you to take a second look and compare the different plans that your employer offers you.

The cost of health insurance has skyrocketed in the last decade. When looking at your health insurance plan, I would encourage you to pay attention to the premiums and deductions. It may seem high or expensive, but remember that you are paying a fraction of the total cost of your health insurance plan. If you had to pay out of pocket for a single, nonsubsidized health insurance plan, you could be paying over $10,000 a year for single coverage and over $25,000 a year for a family of four.

Plans that offer low premiums and high deductibles seem very attractive at first. Your first thought may be to get the health insurance plan with the lowest premium because you are young and healthy. Most of the time, that will work for most people. However, I have seen young, healthy people get an unforeseen illness that requires surgery, and they are left paying thousands of dollars out of pocket because they choose a low-premium, high-deductible plan.

The next thing that you want to check in your health insurance plan options is in- and out-of-network charges. This becomes important when you are choosing your provider. Most health insurance plans cover a certain percentage of the costs if you choose a provider that is in network. The coverage goes down and you have to pay more out-of-pocket expenses if you choose a doctor who is out of network.

The last thing regarding your health insurance is whether your plan is a Preferred Provider Organization (PPO), Health Maintenance Organization (HMO), or other. One of the major distinguishing things between a PPO and HMO is that most HMO plans require referrals in order to see a specialist. It is important to understand all the requirements of the plan that you choose and follow the protocol so you won't be penalized and billed unnecessarily.

Dental insurance is another benefit that can save you a lot of out-of-pocket expenses if you understand and utilize the plan effectively. Dental insurance or nonsubsidized dental plans could cost you thousands of dollars a year. If your employer offers dental insurance, I would suggest you sign up for it because the premiums are generally nominal compared to health insurance premiums. Dental cleanings are usually free and are generally offered twice a year with most plans.

Vision insurance is a nice benefit that is offered by most employers. For a nominal premium cost, you can get an eye exam and discounts for contact lens and glasses. Utilizing your vision insurance can save you hundreds of dollars a year on glasses and over a thousand dollars a year if you include contact lenses.

Life insurance is usually offered by your employer for at least one times your salary at no additional charge to you. Some employers offer more or less than this. Since it is usually a group policy, it usually covers you while you are an employee and are eligible for benefits. As previously mentioned, this life insurance usually ends when your employment ends with your company. You may have an individual term life insurance policy prior to your employment, which usually covers term lengths as short as five years or as long as forty years, but they are typically ten-, twenty- or thirty-year term policies. Some employers offer whole life insurance, but that is rare because it generally costs more money. This is where your financial advisor comes in. They can advise you on which policies are necessary or if additional coverage is needed.

Disability insurance (DI) is a form of insurance that offers income protection when you become disabled and are unable to perform your core work functions. Most employers offer both short-term disability and long-term disability. Some employers offer supplemental long-term disability (LTD), which gives you additional income protection to your LTD benefits.

Short-term disability (STD) insurance can give you partial to full income protection usually for a few months or up to a year. Some short-term disability plans can cover you up to two years in some instances. There is usually a waiting period of thirty to ninety days with most short-term disability plans. Long-term disability (LTD) insurance usually covers serious illness or injuries and can give you partial income protection over one or more years, until the disability ends, or until retirement.

Some employers have started to offer group long-term care insurance. Since you are getting a group rate through your job, this is made available at an affordable premium. These policies generally cover what your health insurance, Medicare, or Medicaid don't cover.

Most people who need long-term care generally spend $50,000 or more annually. Long-term care plans can offer benefits ranging from to three to four years or more and generally cover several hundred thousand dollars for a chronic illness over that defined period of time. These policies generally cover nursing homes, and some cover assisted living facilities. This is something worth discussing with your financial advisor because they know your financial history and have a comprehensive financial plan for you. You generally have a small window to enroll, and then once that period closes, you may not get the opportunity in the future.

Healthcare spending or reimbursement accounts such as a Health Savings Account (HSA), Flexible Spending Account (FSA), and Health Reimbursement Account (HRA) offer you a way to save money in these accounts to pay for covered items such as doctor visits, medical or dental procedures, medications, and other covered items. This benefit can be helpful if you have a scheduled procedure or other costs. The unused portion isn't refundable, but you can generally carry over an amount defined by your employer and the plan.

RETIREMENT BENEFITS

Retirement benefits can be a nice way to build your investments. I would recommend reading and checking your human resources website for updates. There is generally a period that you have to wait before you can enroll in your employer's plan. There may be no waiting period. I have generally seen a one-year waiting period. I would carefully read this section and see if there are any exceptions. If you meet the waiver requirement, I recommend completing the paperwork so you can enroll in your company's plan immediately

Some companies will give you a 5 percent match if you save 5 percent of your earnings. They usually offer this in an after-tax account, such as a Roth Investment Retirement Account (IRA), and pre-tax accounts such as a 401(k) or 403(b). Businesses generally offer a 401(k) plan, and educational institutions and 501(c)(3) tax-exempt organizations generally offer a 403(b) plan. Some employers offer both plans. This is an easy way to save 10 percent of your earnings, so I would recommend taking advantage of this. Having a budget is critical, because following the 50/30/20 rule and my savings tips should easily get you there. If there is no company match but your employer gives you a pension, you have to check with your financial advisor to see if that pension plus social security is enough to get you to your retirement goals.

A well-kept secret is the benefits and perks that you get when you retire from your organization. I would recommend finding out if there are any added benefits that you get rewarded after you have worked a specific number of years for your organization. I would find out if your health, vision, and dental insurance are portable. I would also ask about tuition benefits. I will cover retirement benefits in a whole chapter later on in this book.

TUITION REIMBURSEMENT

Tuition reimbursement is another benefit that some employers offer to assist in their employee's professional development. This benefit alone can cover classes that you take for no charge or a reduced fee semi-annually or annually. This can result in a large amount of savings over time and leave you with more money to invest, pay off your debts, or both.

Using your tuition benefits can be an effective way to earn or complete a degree or certificate program that you have already started taking. For example, if you always wanted a position in the medical field and you already are working for a healthcare system, there may be a way that you can enroll in some of those classes and work toward that degree or certificate. I have watched others do this in the pursuit of their dreams.

OTHER BENEFITS

Some employers offer wellness programs where you get cash back for enrolling in gyms and electronically documenting your visits. Others offer cash back if you get certain metrics measured in your blood annually. You also may get a gym membership, home mortgage, auto loan, parking discounts, a flexible work schedule, and cellular discounts.

Credit

DEFINITION OF CREDIT

Credit can be defined in more than one way. It can be defined as an agreement between a lender and a potential borrower or the creditworthiness of a potential borrower. Having good credit is really important when you are trying to make a large purchase, such as a home or an automobile. Credit is generally measured by a score that is assigned to your creditworthiness. There is more than one credit ranking system. There is the FICO score, which is generally used by banks when they are administering home mortgages or automobile loans. There is also a VantageScore, which was developed by the three credit agencies: TransUnion, Experian, and Equifax. It is used by lenders to measure the credit worthiness of a potential buyer.

FICO scores are used by the majority of lenders. About 90 percent of top lenders use these scores. These scores can range from 300 up to 850. A very poor score is considered in the range of 300 to 499. A poor score is considered in the range of 500 to 600. A fair score is considered in the range of 601 to 660. A good score is considered in the range of 661 up to 780. An excellent or exceptional score is considered in the range from 781 to 850.

When VantageScore came out, they used a different numerical scale than FICO scores. The old VantageScore system used a score range of 501 to 990. The VantageScore system used today by some credit agencies is similar to FICO's numerical system. This new system is called VantageScore 3.0 or 4.0. They both now use the numerical score range of 300 to 850 like the FICO system.

THE 5 CS OF CREDIT

The 5 Cs of credit are character, capacity, capital, collateral, and conditions. Lenders use these characteristics to see if a potential borrower is creditworthy. The first C is character, and it has to do with the applicant's credit history. In other words, does the potential borrower pay their debts on time? The second C is capacity, which is the borrower's debt-to-income ratio. Lenders like to see a low debt-to-income ratio. They prefer a ratio lower than 36 percent, preferably with no more than 28 percent of that amount going toward rent or a mortgage. The lower that ratio is, the higher your credit score will be. The third C is capital, which is the amount of money that the borrower has. Having more money in your financial portfolio is better when you are borrowing from a lender. The fourth C is collateral, which is an asset that can back the loan. It is generally what the lender accepts as a security for a loan. It is a form of protection for the lender in case you as the borrower defaults on the loan. The lender can sell your collateral assets if you default on a loan, so they can recoup the money that was lent to you as the borrower. The fifth C is conditions, which is the purpose of the loan. It includes the amount of principal of the loan and the interest rate. It can also reflect the economy and pending legislative changes.

IMPROVING OR REPAIRING YOUR CREDIT SCORE

There are various things that you can do to repair your credit score or improve your credit score. The most important thing that you can do is to look at your debt-to-income (DTI) ratio. As mentioned earlier, lending institutions like banks like to see a low debt-to-income ratio. So the lower your DTI ratio, generally, the higher your credit score. There are generally two types of DTI ratios that banks consider when they're looking at your debt. The first is called the front-end ratio, which indicates the percentage of your income that goes toward your home mortgage or rent. The second is known as the back-end ratio, which indicates the percentage of your income that goes to car loan payments, credit card payments, student loans, child support payments, alimony payments, and legal judgments.

In summary, DTI ratios are very important determinants of your credit score. For example, if you have a credit limit on one of your credit cards of $1,000 and your credit card balance is $800, which is what you owe the credit card company, you have a lot of credit card debt, which is going to increase your DTI ratio and therefore lower your credit score. If you can reduce that $800 balance to $200 or a zero balance, your credit score can go up as much as ten to twenty points. I have even seen a thirty-point increase in my own credit score in one month after I paid down my credit card balance on one of my credit cards to a zero balance in one month.

EXCELLENT CREDIT AND THE WORLD IT BRINGS YOU

One of the things that having excellent credit allows you to do is to get the best interest rates from banks when you're buying a home or an automobile. Having a lower interest rate allows you to pay off your loan much faster than if you had had a higher interest rate. Paying off your debts faster allows you to have more cash for savings and or investments. The other thing that having excellent credit allows you to do is to use other people's money, namely borrowing money from a bank to make your purchases. This again allows you to have more money for savings and investments and more money to pay your debts down, which puts you one step closer to achieving wealth and being able to leave money to your descendants and generations to come. Wealthy people use this tactic all the time, especially when they're buying real estate. When you have excellent credit and a low DTI ratio, you can buy almost anything you want as long as you have the collateral to support it.

MAINTAIN EXCELLENT CREDIT

Excellent credit is important because it keeps you in a position where you can buy real estate or make other large purchases as long as you have the collateral to back it and you have a low DTI ratio, as I mentioned earlier. Maintaining an excellent credit rating or score means you have to monitor it and make the necessary adjustments to your DTI ratio if your credit score drops. This means that you may have to shift some of your credit card debts to other credit cards in order to keep your credit score in the excellent range. If one of your credit cards' DTI ratio increases above that standard 36 percent that banks like to see, then you're going to have to work hard to get the debt on that credit card down before it lowers your credit score. This is important because your credit score is tied to the interest rate that you're going to get.

I remember when I purchased a car over a decade ago and my credit score was in the fair to good range, I had a higher interest rate on the automobile that I purchased because I didn't have excellent credit. When I was able to understand what my credit score meant and the summary explanations of why I got the credit score that I got from the agency, then I was able to put into action the things that I needed to do to improve my credit score.

It took time to get my credit score up to the excellent to exceptional range. It took months to years of trying to balance my debt and continuing to make my bill payments on time. What really helped me improve my credit score early on was to sign up for a bill pay service with my bank. The reason my credit score wasn't great was because I didn't have a system for paying my bills on time. I would forget to pay my bill and then get a notice about my unpaid bill, and by then, the creditor had already contacted the credit agencies to let them know that I was more than thirty days late. The later you pay your bills, the worse your score will be. It is imperative that you sign up for a bill pay service so you can pay your bills on time. Now that I have a full understanding of how credit scores are calculated and what the different credit scores mean, it is easy for me to make the necessary changes that I need to make to keep my credit score in the excellent to exceptional range.

CHAPTER 5

Retirement

GETTING A FINANCIAL PLANNER: DO I REALLY NEED ONE?

There are many ways in which you can plan for your financial retirement. You can plan by yourself or hire a financial advisor who is certified as a financial planner. This will be money well spent. They will bring many years of wisdom, training, and experience with them. They will help you create a realistic financial plan that is tailored to you and your family's needs. The most important step that you can take is to take action and complete this task. This will put you closer to your retirement goals than if you do this without a certified financial planner and advisor. They will guide you and get you on your way toward saving and investing.

Throughout our lives we will have both short-term and long-term goals that need to be assessed and reviewed. Whether you need to find a good, comprehensive financial plan, pay for your children to attend college, or save for your retirement, you can find the assistance and services of a qualified, certified financial advisor.

A good, certified financial advisor will help lead and guide your decisions throughout the year. Having an advisor doesn't take away the inherent risks of investing. They will help you know if you are close to achieving your financial goals.

Employer plans such as a 401(k) or 403(b) can offer some of the best retirement vehicles for saving. As I mentioned earlier, if you aren't taking your company up on their offer to match your investment in a 401(k) or 403(b), then you should reconsider doing so. That company match invested at least at 6 percent over decades can translate to $100,000 or more in retirement. I know because I have benefited, as have others I know, by not leaving money on the table. When it comes to retirement investing it helps to have a financial advisor guide you along the way.

RETIREMENT PLANS: ROTH IRA VS. 401(K) OR 403(B) OR 457 PLANS

One of my favorite retirement vehicles is a Roth IRA, which is essentially a type of IRA or an after-tax retirement plan. It is basically a tax-sheltered retirement plan for you through your retirement. It has a maximum limit on what you can save annually. If you make under a defined amount which is set by the government, you can save up to $6,000 a year and $7,000 if you are over age fifty. Once you open the account, you have to wait at least five years or be age fifty-nine and a half before you can withdraw any money without paying a 10 percent penalty.

The money in Roth IRAs grows tax free, and no taxes are imposed on withdrawals. The reason is because you effectively paid income taxes and received no tax deduction when you made your deposits. This is in contrast to a traditional IRA, which is tax deductible if you qualify for it. The exceptions to the early withdrawal penalty on Roth IRAs are college expenses, a first home purchase, and the birth or adoption of a child. Because of the global COVID-19 pandemic and the Coronavirus Stimulus Bill in 2020, another exception was added to allow withdrawals up to $100,000 without penalty from both the Roth IRA and traditional IRA.

Another benefit of having a Roth IRA, if you meet the qualifications, is having it function as an emergency savings fund once you are at least fifty-nine and a half years old and able to make tax-free withdrawals. You can withdraw the sum of your contributions at any time without a penalty or tax. If you withdraw investment earnings such as capital gains, interest income, or dividends from your contribution deposits before age fifty-nine and a half, you will be hit with a 10 percent penalty for doing so.

You have fifteen and a half months to accumulate emergency funds to put in a Roth IRA for that year if eligible. It is important to remember not to invest the portion of your Roth IRA that you are planning to keep as an emergency fund. This portion of your Roth IRA that you are keeping for emergency funds should be left in cash so it can be easily liquidated and should be used for events like job loss. That means that this portion of funds that is deemed emergency funds sits in the cash portion of your Roth IRA and isn't invested in stocks, bonds, mutual funds, ETFs, or other investment products. This can be a nice way to use your Roth IRA as an emergency fund if you have depleted your savings account or you just want another emergency fund to access when needed.

You don't need to report Roth IRA contributions on your tax return because they don't affect your taxable income since this is after-tax money and you already paid taxes on it before you invested it. These contributions are considered earned and therefore are tax free. This makes a Roth IRA one of the best savings vehicles available to save toward retirement.

All of this takes discipline, comprehensive planning, and proper advising from your certified financial planner. Withdrawing funds usually takes one business day if the request is made by 4:00 p.m. that day. Wire transfers also can take one business day and will cost a fee. If you are withdrawing money from stocks, it can take up to three business days unless you have a checking account with the institution that holds your Roth IRA.

Another nice feature about a Roth IRA is that they have no required minimum distribution (RMD) rule while you are the account holder and alive. That means you as the account owner have the flexibility to withdraw the money when you see fit to do so or when you have a need. There is a requirement that a distribution be made by your beneficiaries by the end of five years after your death. You can get more details from the IRS at www.irs.gov.

Here are some other retirement savings vehicles. You have a traditional individual retirement account (IRA), 401(k), 401(a), 403(b), and 457(b) plans. A traditional IRA is a retirement savings vehicle that you can establish on your own. There are income and investment limits to this type of account. A 401(k) is a type of employer-sponsored plan that has its own set of rules established by the government. A 401(a) plan is an employer retirement plan that allows investing through dollars or percentages. They typically offer you mutual fund investments. In general, a 403(b) plan offers mutual fund investments plus annuity options. The employer establishes eligibility and the vesting schedule. 401(a) and 403(b) plans are usually offered by universities and/or nonprofit organizations. This is where you check your eligibility in the retirement section of your employee benefits plan. A 457(b) plan is a tax-advantaged employee retirement plan that is offered by local, state, and some nonprofit organizations. All of these plans have investment limits as outlined by the plan.

There are retirement savings vehicles for small businesses. One type is called a Savings Incentive Match Plan for Employees Individual Retirement Account (SIMPLE IRA), which is a tax-deferred retirement plan designed for small businesses with one hundred or fewer employees. It allows both the small business owner or sole proprietor and the employee to make contributions to the plan. It functions like a traditional IRA but has a higher contribution limit. It has a contribution limit of $13,500 for 2021. There is also a catch-up limit of $3,000. If you are over age fifty, you can contribute up to $16,500 a year.

If you are a small business or are self-employed, you can invest in a Simplified Employee Pension (SEP) IRA. This is a tax-deferred plan where the employer makes the contributions directly for the employee. The employer can contribute up to 25 percent of the employee's salary or up to $57,000— whichever is less. Employers don't have to make these contributions annually, which makes it a little different from some of the other retirement vehicles that I mentioned earlier.

In summary, you see that there are many retirement plans, and they all have their own eligibility criteria and rules. It is therefore crucial that you stay abreast of the changes and updates by regularly visiting your human resources handbook, pamphlet, or website. Another good website to visit is the IRS website at www.irs.gov. They have detailed sections about all of these mentioned plans and others including their tax implications and rules for withdrawal.

RETIREMENT GOALS: DO I HAVE ENOUGH MONEY SAVED?

A general retirement rule that many financial advisors use is that you should aim to save at least one times your salary by age thirty, three times your salary by age forty, six times your salary by age fifty, eight times your salary by age sixty, and ten times your salary by age sixty-seven. Other advisors use a rule that says that by age thirty-five you should have one to one and a half times your income. For example, if you earn $50,000 a year and you are thirty-five years old, you should have at least $50,000 to $75,000 saved if you started saving at age twenty-five.

These are general guidelines that you can use to see if your retirement savings is on track. A down economy or a bear market in which stock prices are falling can also impact your retirement savings. If your estimates fall short, you can always increase your retirement savings in your 401(k) or 403(b) as long as you don't exceed the government limits. Catch-up contributions allow people who are age fifty or older to save more in a retirement plan. This is what I had to do because my retirement savings were below the recommended guidelines for my age.

TIMING: WHEN SHOULD I RETIRE?

Retirement is a big decision and life change with which we will all be faced. No one knows the ideal time to retire but you and your financial planner. Retirement planning, just like financial planning, should involve your significant other if you have one and a certified financial planner. This is not an easy decision because your goals and finances can change over time. For example, you may plan on retiring at the age of sixty-seven because at that age you will be eligible to collect your full retirement social security benefits. You may also pick this age because you expect to have more money saved in retirement, remembering that most people prepare to withdraw at least 80 percent of their annual pre-retirement salary every year while in retirement. In other words, your annual income at age sixty-six is $100,000. At age sixty-seven, you plan to retire, and it is suggested by most financial planners that you will need about $80,000 a year to live on. That number can be adjusted down if you include social security income, and you have minimal debts going into retirement.

Some people retire at age forty or fifty because of good financial planning, investments, inheritances, and living below their means. Yes, this can be accomplished if you create a budget and stick to it. This means buying the things that you need, which usually accounts for about 50 percent of your budget as mentioned earlier. This also means limiting your wants, which is usually about 30 percent of your budget, and increasing your savings and debt management, which is usually 20 percent of your budget. If you start financial planning in your twenties and you follow the advice of your certified financial planner, you may be able to accomplish this.

If you reach age forty or fifty and you decide you want to continue to work, save, and invest more, then you reassess that goal and change it if needed. The same thing applies if you want to retire at age fifty-five, sixty, sixty-two, sixty-seven, or seventy. No matter what age you pick to retire, you have to be able to sustain yourself for the decades to come.

Some people continue to work and defer retirement so they can keep their health insurance while saving more money for retirement. Health insurance and medical expenses tend to increase as we age. It is one of the most expensive costs that could chip away at your budget if you retire before age sixty-five. This is one of the major reasons why most people work until age sixty-five, when they will be eligible for the federal health insurance program called Medicare.

There is no magical age to retire these days, especially if you have a comprehensive financial plan and certified financial planner. I will keep reiterating these concepts because they are key to your transition into retirement. Men retire at an average age of sixty-four and women at an average age of sixty-two. If your debts are paid and you have calculated that you have enough to retire and live off of, then it may make sense for you to retire. You may love your job and working in your profession but may desire to retire so you can have more time to yourself and your family.

RETIREMENT LIVING

Deciding where to live in retirement is part of your retirement planning with your certified financial planner and significant other if you have one. Some people move to a city or suburb when they are young and planning for a family so they can be near the best schools. You may want to move out of that area after your children go off to college and you no longer want a large house to manage in your retirement years.

Downsizing and moving to another city or state sounds reasonable in your retirement years. Maybe you want to move to a state that has a warmer climate or more affordable housing. There are lots of retirement communities that are being built all over the country. Maybe you want a lower tax burden in your retirement years. These are all valid reasons to move and get a fresh start in retirement. You have so many options available to you if you choose to move.

CHAPTER 6

Estate Planning

ADVANCED HEALTHCARE DIRECTIVE

Financial advisors usually advise getting estate planning, but since legal documents are involved, it is best to get estate planning set up by an attorney. An advanced healthcare directive, also known as a living will, personal directive, or medical directive, is an essential part of estate planning. It includes a durable power of attorney for healthcare and other advanced care planning documents. It allows you to express your values and desires related to end-of-life care.

A living will is a written document that helps you communicate your wishes and desires to your healthcare providers. It allows you to communicate how you want to be cared for if you are dying or unconscious and unable to make your own decisions.

A durable power of attorney for healthcare is a legal document that names a proxy, which is someone who can make medical decisions for you when you are unable to make them for yourself. The person that you choose as your proxy should know and understand your beliefs, wishes, and values since they will be expected to make medical decisions for you when you are unable to. A proxy can be chosen in addition to a living will or instead of a living will.

The types of decisions that will need to be made include medical issues such as Do Not Resuscitate (DNR) orders and organ and tissue donation. Another consideration is whether or not to donate your brain to scientific research. This helps researchers learn more about certain types of diseases and how we might better prevent and treat them in the future.

POWER OF ATTORNEY

A power of attorney is a legal document that allows a principal to appoint someone known as the agent to act on their behalf should they become incapacitated. This agent should be someone you know and trust, since they would be acting on your behalf. A power of attorney can be used for many things. It can give the agent power to make financial transactions, sign legal documents, or make healthcare decisions if the principal is incapacitated. The agent can only make decisions as outlined in the legal document. The power of attorney usually expires when you die unless you set an expiration date. Lastly, power of attorney doesn't override a will.

PROBATE

Probate is the legal or court-supervised process where a will is reviewed to determine whether it is authentic and valid. In other words, it is the proving of a will. It is also the general administering of a deceased person's will or estate without a will and the legal process through which a deceased person's property is transferred after they die. During this process, the assets of the deceased person are gathered, debts are paid off, and the remaining assets are distributed in accordance with an estate plan and the law. This process generally takes between four and eight months, but it can sometimes take one to two years. It is recommended that you seek an attorney to assist you with probate.

WILLS AND TRUSTS

A will is a written document that expresses the wishes of the deceased person. These wishes can include the naming of assets and whom they are left for. It becomes active after one's death. A trust is another method of estate transfer. It becomes active and effective the day it is created. The grantor of a trust can list the distribution of their assets before their death.

There are two types of trusts. An irrevocable trust can't be changed or altered after it is created. These are often created for tax purposes. Living trusts, however, can be changed by the grantor after they are created. They are created while the trustor or property owner is alive. Revocable living trusts are primarily created in order to avoid probate. They may be changed during the life of the trustor or property owner. The trustor maintains ownership of the property that is held in trust while the trustor or property owner is alive.

Whether you decide to get a will or a trust, it is generally recommended that you seek legal, tax, and investment advice. In other words, you should consult with an attorney and certified financial planner for estate planning. Like a will, a trust will require the transfer of property after the death of a loved one. In summary, one of the benefits of a trust, unlike a will, is that you can transfer property without having to go to probate court. It costs money to set up a trust and it is well worth it because you can rack up fees and spend months to years going through probate court. The heirs of the estate usually end up paying these fees, which could cost up to 7 percent of the total value of the estate.

Estate planning seems like it can be an unnecessary expense at first, but think about how beneficial it can be to you and your heirs. They can get your property transferred to them without having to go through the time and expense of probate court. It is also helpful having an attorney and financial planner involved so they can help you plan for and minimize the taxes that are usually involved when property is transferred.

CHAPTER

7

Debt Management

DEBT AND YOUR CREDIT SCORE

One of the biggest factors that affects your credit score is carrying a lot of debt, especially high credit card debt. About 30 percent of your credit score comes from the amount of debt that you are carrying. Your credit report lists all your debts along with your credit limit. Having a high debt ratio makes it very difficult to get new credit cards, credit limit increases, and other loans.

It is recommended that you pay your debts in full so your credit score won't be impacted. Anytime you settle a debt and pay part of the debt back in a repayment, that will impact and lower your credit score. Settled debt also gets reported as settled and is reported on your credit report. Accounts generally remain on your credit report for up to ten years when they are closed in good standing. Any positive payments or paid in full status will strengthen your credit score.

DEBT MANAGEMENT PLAN

There are debt management plans (DMP) that are available when you are struggling to pay your debts and bills. Getting on these plans will impact your credit score and ultimately lower it. When you set up an agreement with your creditor, you are usually paying reduced payments. The original payments remain on your credit report so lenders can see this when you go to apply for credit. A lower credit score translates into you being a potential high-risk borrower to lenders. This is important to keep in mind if you have a large purchase such as a home mortgage or car purchase.

BACK TO THE BUDGET PLAN

Remember that your budget plan usually comprises about 50 percent needs, 30 percent wants, and 20 percent savings and debts. One way to tackle debt is to cut back spending in one of the above areas, preferably your wants and not your needs. I used this as a strategy to help pay down my debts over time. You should be able to create extra savings by utilizing the budgeting tips that I mentioned earlier like using points to make purchases instead of cash, coupons, and other savings methods. You can now apply the extra money to your debt category. It is important to save and pay your debts at the same time so you can ultimately achieve debt freedom. Not having debt really frees your cash for more investing and wealth creation, which is your ultimate goal.

OTHER STRATEGIES FOR PAYING DEBTS

The first step in managing debt is to create a list of all of your debts, including credit card, student loan, mortgage, and car loan. The most important and largest debt if you own a house is your mortgage. You have to pay this, or you will be in jeopardy of losing your house. The next recommended strategy is either to pay off the debt with the highest interest rate or pay off the smallest debt first. For example, if you have a credit card and the balance is $1,000 with an interest rate of 22 percent, then you may want to start paying that card down first, especially if your other credit card or loan has a balance of $1,000 but has an interest rate of 9 percent. The 9 percent debt will grow at a slower rate than the 22 percent debt. Once you pay that debt off, you take that payment amount and apply it to any remaining debt until you pay all of your debts off. I have applied this strategy to my large student loan debt, and it works. I had about seven student loans at one point, and I started paying off the smallest debt first because they all had similar interest rates.

Another strategy to paying debts off is to have it automatically debited from your checking account every month. Some guarantors will give you a discount on the interest rate if you do this monthly. Other lenders will give you a discount, usually 1 percent off the loan, especially if you make thirty-six months of on-time payments. I was able to get this discount with one of my lenders after I consolidated the loan and made thirty-six months of on-time payments. When you have a lot of student loan debt, 1 percent off of the loan over years of payments can translate into hundreds to thousands of dollars in savings.

Another popular strategy that turns a thirty-year mortgage into a twenty-three-year mortgage is to pay an extra monthly payment every year or pay biweekly payments. Some banks can set this up at no extra charge, but others will charge you to set up biweekly payments. It also helps you achieve equity in your house faster. Having more equity in your house will also make you eligible for a home equity loan or line of credit, which can be used for home improvement or repairs in the future.

When you need immediate help with your debts, there are nonprofit credit counseling agencies that can help you manage your debts. You can usually get a free consultation, and then if you need any other services, you will be charged a fee. Debt can be very overwhelming, so any time you feel you need help, reach out to debt management companies or agencies.

ACHIEVING DEBT FREEDOM

Debt freedom is one of the most important steps that puts you on the path to wealth accumulation. You can't effectively get to wealth accumulation and generational wealth if you are saddled with debt. Debt is like a weight, and it brings anxiety and worry with it. Achieving debt freedom should parallel you working toward wealth accumulation. Paying off your debts frees up your cash for savings, investments, and retirement.

Imagine waking up debt free. You don't have a care in the world or anxiety over how you are going to pay your bills. It is a great feeling. It would give you the freedom to choose what you want to do or how you plan your day. You no longer have to worry about screening your phone calls or not answering the phone. All of this should allow you to enjoy your life more and increase your sense of financial freedom.

Waking up one day debt free is like a dream. You can get there by sticking to and reevaluating your budget. If your debts start to grow, cut back on the things that you want— that 30 percent of your budget—and work toward paying your debts down. That extra bag, pair of shoes, flat-screen TV, or truck that you think you need won't give you half of the joy that you will have when you can breathe a sigh of relief from being saddled with debt.

Achieving debt freedom is such an accomplishment. We don't celebrate this accomplishment nearly as much as when someone earns more money. The freedom and the peace of mind that you get is priceless. You will have less anxiety and worry because there are no debts to pay. You should be able to fund the things that you enjoy, like traveling or taking up that hobby that you once pursued.

CHAPTER 8

Investments

INVEST IN YOURSELF

It is important to invest in yourself if you are planning to achieve the goal of wealth accumulation and generational wealth. This may be the most profitable investment that you ever make. When you have the opportunity to take a class or pursue a degree, you should take it. This is one of the best ways to ensure a brighter future by investing in your personal and professional growth.

By expanding your knowledge and developing your mind, you should be able to personally and professionally grow and move to the next level. This is where your tuition employee benefits can be useful and effective. You can take a class in your area of expertise so you can enhance your knowledge and skills. You can also attend conferences, lectures, and workshops or take online courses as another way of utilizing available training.

Another way that you can expand your knowledge is by reading books and articles. You can acquire information through TED talks, YouTube, and other social media outlets.

You can also get information from newsletters, bulletins, publications, blogs, and vlogs.

Anytime you do something creative, you are learning and growing inside. There are so many ways that you can use creativity, such as reading, writing, cooking, learning a new language, gardening, dancing to music, or designing clothing. All of these different forms of creativity can enhance and develop your mind, so it is important to do something creative regularly.

INVEST IN YOUR CHILD

There are two different types of IRAs that can be set up for children. There is the traditional IRA and Roth IRA. With the Roth IRA, you pay the taxes when you put the money into the account, so the funds that are the contributions and earnings are considered after-tax money. The money grows tax free in both the traditional IRA and the Roth IRA. The difference is that when the child withdraws the money, decades later or in retirement, they won't have to pay taxes on it. There are also no required minimum distributions (RMDs), just like in the Roth IRA for adults.

Yes, you can open a Roth IRA for your child. This is useful because it is a tax-advantaged savings vehicle that has time and the power of compounding to help it mature through the decades.

Your child, regardless of age, can contribute to an IRA provided that they have earned income according to the IRS guidelines. Others can contribute as long as they don't exceed the amount of the child's earned income. Lastly, the IRA has to be set up us a custodial account by a parent or other adult.

It makes sense to open a Roth IRA for your child since they don't earn enough to benefit from the up-front tax deduction that you get with a traditional IRA. The Roth IRA is also the preferred savings vehicle for children because they are likely to be in a higher tax bracket in decades to come since they are saving as a child. If that child keeps their Roth IRA until age fifty-nine and a half, any withdrawals will be tax free.

When you open a Roth IRA, the account has to be in the child's name and social security number. The law requires that the custodian make all of the investment decisions until that child is over age eighteen or over age nineteen or twenty-one in other states. Once the child isn't considered a minor, you as the custodian have to turn the account over to them.

A 529 college savings plan is a tax-advantaged investment vehicle in the United States that is designed to encourage saving for future higher education expenses of a designated beneficiary, such as your child. You must use the funds for education, and there are limitations on state tax benefits. There are, however, federal income tax benefits and sometimes state benefits. These plans incur fees. They are generally flexible but this isn't a self-directed investment plan. One of the drawbacks of this plan is that if it isn't used for qualified educational expenses, you'll have to pay both federal income taxes and a 10 percent penalty.

Life insurance is a form of investment for an event for which no one expects to plan. You can purchase whole life insurance for your child, which includes a death benefit. It is another way that you can invest in your child and create an account that can be used as cash for college or a down payment on a house if the death benefit isn't used.

Although whole life insurance policies build cash value, the rate of return is generally lower than a 529 college savings plan. It is still a good investment because it builds financial value for your child in the future. It should also be looked at as a way to augment any other savings vehicles that the family has.

TYPES OF INVESTMENTS

Stocks, Bonds, Mutual Funds, Exchange-Traded Funds (ETF), Annuities, Derivatives, and Hedge Funds

There are several types of marketable securities in which you can invest. Securities are defined as financial instruments that hold value and that can be traded between parties. There are four types of securities: equity securities, debt securities, derivative securities, and a combination of equity and debt securities.

An example of an equity security is capital stock, which includes shares of both common and preferred stock. They give stockholders a share of ownership in a company, partnership, or trust. Owning a stock is a way for an investor to profit from the success of a publicly traded company, such as Apple or Amazon, with which most of us are familiar. For example, if you purchase stock in a company, as an equity holder, you purchase shares believing that that company will perform well, and as a result, the value of those shares you purchased will increase.

Debt securities are a financial instrument that allows you to have a stake in a loan to a company, organization, or governmental agency. There are various types of debt securities. Corporate bonds are a type of debt security that is issued by a firm and sold to investors. In this transaction, the company gets the capital or money that it needs to run their business, and the investor gets paid a pre-established number of interest payments at either a variable or fixed interest rate. Most bonds pay dividends like stocks do and mostly pay them at maturity or at a defined period of time, like semi-annually. This means that you can buy a corporate bond, and as a bondholder you essentially lend money with interest.

Another type of investment vehicle is the mutual fund. A mutual fund is a collection or portfolio of stocks, bonds, or other types of securities which is overseen by a fund manager. The fund manager is a professional money manager who manages that fund. When you purchase a mutual fund share, you are investing in a company that is pooling money from many investors and buying hundreds to sometimes thousands of securities, such as stocks, bonds, and short-term debt. Mutual funds are a popular type of investment security because they allow you to have a diversified portfolio. That diversified portfolio could include companies that you may know and already believe are going to perform well. They also give you a professional management team, affordability, and liquidity.

An exchange-traded fund (ETF) is a collection of securities that trade on an exchange, just like a stock. They have similar characteristics to a stock. The difference is that as a shareholder in a company, you own part of that company, whereas when you purchase an ETF, you purchase a portion of the collection of assets from the ETF provider. Those assets can include stocks, bonds, commodities, or currencies. They are usually affordable and diversified, and that is what makes them attractive as a type of security to invest in. ETFs trade with the ease of a stock, but also give you the diversification benefits of a mutual fund. They generally have lower fees than other fund types. For example, the administrative expense or expense ratio charged for owning shares in a specific mutual fund usually averages around 0.5 percent and can go as high as almost 2 percent. That number can be as low as 0.18 percent in an index equity ETF. They can have varying risks like stocks and mutual funds.

Annuities are insurance contracts that are issued and distributed by financial institutions. The funds are invested with the goal of paying out fixed income later in a person's life. They can be structured as fixed, variable, immediate, or deferred income. They are often used to fund retirement, especially when there is concern that a person may outlive their savings. They can also be created to turn a large lump sum of money, such as lottery winnings or large cash settlements from a lawsuit, into regular cash flow.

Derivatives are securities that get their value from an underlying asset or benchmark. For example, some common derivatives include futures contracts, options, forwards, and swaps. They are used by institutions to speculate on price changes in the underlying asset. For example, you can purchase an option, which is a contract, that allows you to invest in the market, while committing less money than would be required if you purchased the stock. Most derivatives aren't traded on exchanges like stocks and ETFs. Most trade over the counter (OTC). This type of trading is considered high-risk investing and is definitely not for the faint of heart.

Last but not least, we need to talk about hedge funds. A hedge fund is a pooled investment company that is able to do more complex trading than non-hedge funds. They are typically structured as limited partnerships. Third-party investors like pension funds, banks, and wealthy individuals invest in the partnership as limited partners. The hedge fund management group or team serves as the general partner.

Hedge funds do complex trading in an attempt to improve the performance of the hedge fund. Some of these techniques are known as short selling, leverage, and derivatives. They essentially invest their client's money in these complex, alternative investments with the strategy of trying to beat the market or provide a hedge against unforeseen market changes. Thus, they are called hedge funds because they are hedging in their strategies, and they aren't available to the average investor.

RETIREMENT AND GENERAL INVESTMENTS

Now that you have basic information about the different types of investments that can be used for retirement or general investing, what is the next step? I just listed the different types of available investments that are used by most investors above. I did this so you would be aware of the different types of investment vehicles that are available to you.

It is recommended that you get a certified financial planner and a financial advisor who is certified and has experience with investments. There is a lot to know and understand when it comes to investing, so you want a professional to give you advice. I would advise that you get comfortable with the different types of investment products so when you meet with them, you will know and understand the terminology that they use.

It is so important that you start investing as soon as you are able to because it takes time to grow your investments. You can't expect, as an average investor, to invest $1,000 today and have $1,000,000 tomorrow. It takes time and a good investment strategy to increase your earnings over time. If you start investing at a young age and you contribute to that investment regularly over time, it is quite possible to have a nice nest egg in retirement.

THE PRINCIPLES OF SMART INVESTMENTS

The first principle to smart investing is to know and understand your investment style. This is a question that a financial advisor will ask you when you meet with them. They will ask you if you prefer having an aggressive investment portfolio, which means that you can take big drops in your portfolio when the market is down, or if you have a more conservative investment style. It is important to know your investment goals and the time frame that you expect to achieve them. For example, you should have an idea of what age and an estimation of how much money you would like in retirement.

It is recommended that you invest as early as possible. Getting a start in investing in your twenties gives you a lot more time to grow your portfolio. The earlier you start investing, the better. Generally, the longer you wait to get started, the more you will need to invest to get to the same retirement age and goal.

Another good investment strategy to adopt is to invest regularly. It is even better if you are able to increase the amount without going over your plan limit.

Matching what your employer invests in your portfolio is another option. For example, some employers will invest 5 percent of your salary if you invest 5 percent of your salary. This strategy can get you closer to your goal. If you don't take advantage of this strategy, you could be losing a large amount of money over time.

You can also consider building a diversified portfolio. A diversified portfolio is a mixture of investment products, such as stocks, bonds, money market securities, mutual funds, and ETFs. You can consider investment products with varying risks. I would advise you to do this with a financial advisor.

It is so important to log into your account regularly and monitor your portfolio. This will keep you up to date on what is going on in your account. If you have large losses or your portfolio is lagging behind the market, you should be aware of that so you can review your portfolio with your financial advisor to see if you need to make any changes.

REAL ESTATE

Investing in real estate can be a great strategy for building wealth and diversifying your investment portfolio. You can make money as an investor through the rental income, appreciation of the property, and profits generated by business activity on the property.

There are three basic strategies for real estate investment. You can invest in a Real Estate Investment Trust (REIT), which provides real estate exposure without you financing, owning, or operating the property. Other strategies include becoming a landlord of a rental property and buying undervalued real estate, fixing it up, and flipping it to sell for a profit. No matter which strategy you choose, they all work, and you can be successful doing any of them once you understand and master the process.

The first piece of real estate that we all strive to acquire is a home for ourselves and family in which to live. Buying a home is a process and it takes time unless you have money for a cash sale. Most people don't buy their homes with cash, so they have to go through the mortgage process, which can take time and patience.

The first thing that you need to look at if you are going to get a mortgage is your credit. Again, this is the FICO score that credit agencies assign you based on your credit worthiness. In other words, do you pay your bills on time and pay off debts that you borrow? Are you late on your payments or carry high revolving debt? Is your debt-to-income ratio high? The answers to all of these questions impact your credit score.

When you are buying a house, low is any score under 620. Fair to good is a credit score between 620 and 740. Banks really want to see a score of 740 and higher. When you have a FICO score of 740 or higher, that tells the bank that you pay your bills on time and that you repay your bills. You are more likely to get a mortgage with the lowest possible interest rate when you have excellent credit. A lower score tells the bank that you are not as trustworthy and therefore have them wonder why they should lend you the money. You may get a mortgage with a score lower than 740, but you will be penalized with a higher interest rate. Banks don't like to give loans or mortgages to individuals who are less likely to pay them back.

So whether you are buying your own home or a rental property for investment purposes, you will need to have excellent credit to get those mortgages and loans approved at the lowest possible interest rate. Credit plays a major role in our life, so we must always be cognizant of it when we are making purchases and paying our bills and debts. Credit, along with budgeting and investing, plays a key role in your journey toward wealth accumulation and generational wealth. Having an excellent credit score makes the journey less bumpy.

Taxes

DEFINITION OF TAXES

A tax is the amount of money that you have to pay to the government. It is something an individual or company pays as part of their income or profits to the government. The government, in turn, uses that money to repair roads and to provide goods and services to others. Some of the largest goods and services include Medicare and Social Security.

GET A CERTIFIED PUBLIC ACCOUNTANT (CPA)

According to Investopedia, "a Certified Public Accountant (CPA) is a designation given by the American Institute of Certified Public Accountants (AICPA) to individuals that meet the educational requirements and pass the Uniform CPA Examination." This examination and title help to enforce the professional standards in this industry. It is important that you check the credentials of an accountant during the vetting process so you know that they are certified.

Your CPA should be doing your taxes. In order to get the best assessment of your taxes, you should get a bookkeeper in addition to a CPA. I would also recommend keeping track of your donations and receipts for potential deductions.

UNDERSTANDING TAXES

It is best to go to the IRS website at www.irs.gov to get the tax code and information. Any new rules or acts that are passed will be updated on their website. I would also recommend going to your state and local government website to read the tax code and to get updated information on changes. If you have any additional questions, you can ask your CPA, who should be doing your taxes.

TYPES OF TAXES

There are many types of taxes that an individual or a business has to pay. There are sales taxes, local taxes, state taxes, federal taxes, and interest and dividends taxes. There are nine states where you don't pay an income tax. Those states include Alaska, Florida, Nevada, New Hampshire, South Dakota, Tennessee, Texas, Washington, and Wyoming. Four states have no statewide sales tax, and they are Delaware, New Hampshire, Oregon, and Montana. Alaska has no statewide sales tax, but it allows cities and towns to levy a sales tax. New Hampshire is the only state that doesn't have sales or state taxes. It does, however, tax interest and dividends at 5 percent.

There are three federal taxes that are imposed on wage and salary income. They are income taxes, Medicare, and Social Security. The Federal Insurance Contributions Act

(FICA) is deducted from each paycheck. As you work and pay FICA, you earn credits toward Social Security Benefits, which you can start collecting at age sixty-two, sixty-seven, seventy, or the designated age based on your birth date.

MINIMIZING TAXES

There are several ways that you can minimize your taxes. The first one, which we have spent a lot of time talking about, is contributing to a retirement account. You want to look at the types of retirement accounts that allow you to save with pre-tax dollars, such as a 401(k), 403(b), and 401(a). You can also open a Health Savings Account (HSA). You can still contribute to an IRA or Roth IRA if you are eligible for it. You can also donate to your church or charities. Check with your CPA, since there were several changes to the tax code in 2018 that limit certain deductions.

Creating Generational Wealth

ADOPT A WEALTHY MINDSET AND LIFESTYLE

One thing to remember is that the rich have a lot of money, and the wealthy don't worry about it. Accumulating wealth requires goals, but keeping your money requires a rich mindset. The lifestyle that you acquire is a lifestyle of health, gratitude, helping others, and giving back.

There are some basic wealth accumulation tips that are helpful to remember. The first basic fact is that if you invest $1 a day at an interest rate of 10 percent compounded daily, you will have $1,000,000 in fifty-six years. That amount will vary depending on the interest rate that you earn over time. Yes, you can save $1 a day, $30 a month, or $365 a year invested at an interest rate of 10 percent over fifty-six years and be a millionaire.

A DOLLAR A DAY GROWS INTO $1 MILLION

Interest Rate	Time in Years
3%	147
5%	100
10%	56
15%	40
20%	32

A DOLLAR A DAY GROWS INTO $1 MILLION

If one family member could do this, just imagine how much different their life could be after fifty-six years of saving and investing. If every family member were able to do this and then start this investment process with the birth of their children, they can start the process of developing generational wealth.

If you can save for sixty-six years at interest rates varying from 0 percent to 20 percent, you could have even more money for retirement and the next generation. Investing $1 a day at a 3 percent interest rate will give you $77,000 in sixty-six years. Investing $1 a day at a 10 percent interest rate will give you $2.7 million dollars in sixty-six years. Yes, you will have saved an additional $1.7 million dollars by extending your savings from fifty-six years to sixty-six years. Investing $1 a day for sixty-six years at a 15 percent interest rate will give you $50 million in sixty-six years, and at a 20 percent interest rate, $1 billion in sixty-six years. Yes, it is possible to save and invest at least $1 billion in your lifetime. Implementing and using this strategy requires diligence, consistency, and patience.

A DOLLAR A DAY COMPOUNDED AT VARIOUS RATES FOR SIXTY-SIX YEARS

Interest Rate	Cumulative Savings
0%	$24,000
3%	$77,000
5%	$193,000
10%	$2.7 million
15%	$50 million
20%	$1 billion

INVESTING IN YOURSELF

Investing in yourself through the different vehicles such as retirement investments, savings, and real estate are great ways to build wealth and leave a legacy for your family. Another way that you can invest in yourself and the legacy that you will be leaving is to become an entrepreneur and start your own business. You can invest in yourself by taking classes, earning a degree or certificate, or doing the things that you are passionate about. Investing in yourself can be used as a way to create wealth.

INVESTING IN YOUR CHILDREN

There are several ways that you can invest in your children. You can invest in their education by opening a 529 educational savings account. This is one popular way that you can save for college and use the funds for your child's tuition. You can also open a whole life insurance plan with a death benefit. The life insurance plan can function both as a life insurance plan and as cash for college when needed. In other words, you can open a whole life policy on your infant, toddler, or child and then cash out the policy when they are ready to start college. The cash value can be $20,000 or more depending upon the policy that you take out.

If you have a business and you are the sole owner of the business, you can put your children on payroll. The provisions for child labor, minimum wage, hours, and overtime pay are outlined in the Fair Labor Standards Act of 1938. There are different regulations for children under age fourteen, children ages fourteen and fifteen, and children between the ages of fifteen and eighteen.

You, as the adult, can open a Roth IRA for your child using their name and social security number on the account, and the money that they earn can be invested in a Roth IRA if they qualify for and satisfy the income requirements. You, as the parent, will be a custodial over the account and invest for the child until they are of age, which is usually between eighteen and twenty-one depending on the statute.

One other thing you can do is to open a credit card in your child's name. This will help them build credit and increase their credit score if they pay their bills on time and keep their debt under 20 to 30 percent. The lower that percentage is, the higher the credit score will go. Paying your debts on time and preferably in full is a good habit to develop. When you carry a balance, you will incur interest on the balance, and as a result, the amount that you owe will continue to increase until you pay that balance off.

CREATING MULTIPLE STREAMS OF INCOME

When you are accumulating and building wealth, it is important to look at the concept of multiple streams of income. This is a strategy, tip, and secret that is used by many wealthy individuals. They create more than one stream of income so they can reach their financial goals. You can start by looking at your passions and the things that you enjoy doing. For example, if you enjoy baking cookies and cakes, you can start a side business doing that. If you already have one stream of income, whether that is a full-time or part-time job, you now have a second stream of income. Another stream of income can be through buying and selling online. Another stream of income can be selling products or services.

When you create these streams of income, make sure that you have the necessary licenses, insurances, Employer Identification Number (EIN) or Federal Tax ID number, and anything else needed to set up a business. I have seen many people successfully do this, so you can too. This tried-and-true principle works. The extra income that you generate can go a long way in generating income and ultimately investments over time.

TEACHING THESE WEALTH PRINCIPLES AND GIVING BACK

It is important to teach these wealth principles and be an example to your children. When you give to charity events, you should take your children with you and explain to them why you are donating your money or volunteering your time. I watched my mother give back to her church when I was a child growing up. She volunteered her time and donated 10 percent of her money to her church and different charities.

Some creative ways to give back include fundraising and serving at a food bank. You can make it a quarterly or annual family event so you can support your charitable event as a family. You will get doubly blessed by giving and supporting your charity or community as a family unit. There is power and strength in working together as a family unit toward the greater good of mankind.

As you spend time with your family and children, it is important to have the money talk. Most of what we know and learn about money really comes from what we saw our parents say or do. Any budgeting tips, investment strategies, real estate investing, and estate planning strategies come from what we learned from our parents. As we live and experience life, our colleagues, friends, and associates can also influence our money mindset and thinking about finances.

As I reflect back and look at the influence that my parents had on my relationship with money and my money mindset, I think about the things that impacted me the most. My mother saved $11,000 in cash to put down on the first house in which we ever lived. Homes were much cheaper back then, but the interest rates were much higher on a mortgage. That money would probably translate into $40,000 today. I thought to myself, "How did she come up with that money? Nurses only made about $11,000 to $15,000 a year."

My mother was a master at budget planning and saving money. I watched my mother spend $20 on groceries, and it seemed like there was $1 worth of groceries in each of the twenty bags that we had to unpack. My mother would use couponing to the extreme in order to save money. I could always tell when something was on sale. For example, if I saw four of an item of which she would normally buy one, I knew that it had to be a very good sale going on. That was one of the budgeting tips that I learned from my mother.

Another tip that I learned from my mother was buying clothing on sale or from a discount store. If you wanted extra savings, you bought your clothes off-season. You bought your winter clothes at the end of winter or early spring and then wore them the following winter. The same principle applies to spring and summer clothes. This was how my mother created savings and used the money that she saved to pay off her debts and buy bonds.

My mother didn't tell me about other types of retirement benefits because you can only teach what you know. She was born in South America, and her mother died when she was nineteen years old. Her mother didn't pass along any knowledge about savings or investments, so my mother had to learn it on her own. She moved to London, England, to go to nursing school and then immigrated to the United States when I was a little kid.

I heard my mother talking about buying a franchise in my younger days. She also talked about buying an apartment building and renting it out to college students. She figured if she had to pay for my housing in college, why shouldn't she make money doing it? My mother developed an entrepreneurial spirit. My father, on the other hand, did not. He thought that maintaining a building with tenants was a problem. What he didn't know was that you can buy the apartment building and hire a management company or team to manage the building.

Listening to my mother's dreams definitely inspired me as I grew to understand the principles of money and wealth accumulation. My mother never used the term "multiple streams of income," but now that I look back and reflect on her life, I realize that is what she was trying to achieve. She worked as a nurse but realized that in order to save and accumulate wealth, she had to save and look at ways to invest. This has to be where my love of real estate comes from. I want to pick up her mantle and fulfill that desire to own real estate—and lots of it. All of this is part of my ultimate dream of generational wealth and being able to teach others the importance of it and of creating a legacy for the next generation.

TRANSFERRING WEALTH TO THE NEXT GENERATION

Generational wealth refers to any asset that is passed down to children or grandchildren. It takes careful planning and thoughtful sharing of your goals and intentions along with good investing in the right products. That is the major goal that you want to achieve in your lifestyle. Most of us didn't hear much about this growing up in our households unless it was already a part of our lifestyle. We should always be thinking about generational wealth, even if we don't have children. Generational wealth is a mindset. It is a way of thinking, and we should always be thinking about our children and our future. This is how the Rockefeller's and other wealthy families have left a legacy to their children and grandchildren.

The Rockefeller family is an American industrial, banking, and political family who owns one of the world's largest fortunes. They are still enjoying their fortune while they continue to pass it along to their descendants. If we could strive to build and accumulate wealth, we also could leave a legacy to our children and grandchildren. Although this process takes time and it may even take more than one generation to accomplish this, it can be done. Remember that this process works best when started earlier in life and sustained through-out the lifetime of the person who is doing it. Doing this with a positive mindset and gratitude will make the journey more pleasant and less bumpy. Build a comprehensive plan with your financial advisor, review it periodically, and stay the course on the journey.

Let's get started using these tips and principles so we can leave a legacy to the next generation.

References

1. Harvard Health Publishing, November 22, 2011.

2. "The Five Cs of Credit," Troy Segal, updated May 18, 2021.

3. Will Kenton, "Certified Public Accountant (CPA)," Investopedia, updated August 4, 2021, https://www.investopedia.com/terms/c/cpa.asp.

4. Internal Revenue Service, http://www.irs.gov.

5. Robert G. Allen, *Multiple Streams of Income*, Second Edition, 2005.

A Note to the Reader

Dear Financially Free,

Thank you for reading my first book and going on this journey with me. When I decided to write this book, I wanted to share some secrets and tips that I learned about finances while going through and dealing with the massive debt that I incurred during medical school. I also wanted to give every woman the opportunity to read this book, learn something, and share that with someone else so we can always be learning and growing together.

I would encourage you to start your mornings with a positive mindset and to journal the things for which you are grateful. Develop a heart of gratitude and a life practicing it. It has been shown that being grateful makes us happier and improves our self-esteem. It also improves our relationships and increases our physical and psychological well-being. It reduces stress and helps us sleep. All of these can really get you in a positive money mindset, which is really needed in order to successfully navigate this pathway to wealth accumulation.

Fear not as you go on this journey. Know that others have gone before you and have successfully achieved their goals. Stay focused and see yourself at the finish line. It is a process, and it will take time to get to your destination. Be patient and know that you will get there. Just know that when you get there, you won't be alone. Your children and family will be with you. They will be waiting there for you to pass the baton unto them. They will be smiling, laughing, and crying all at the same time. They will be feeling emotional and overjoyed that you stayed the course and you made it.

You will get to the finish line, and you will do this. You will be the first one in your family to build wealth and pass it along to your descendants. How cool will that be to know that you got there using this C.R.E.D.I.T. system that I developed for you? Remember C is for credit, R is for retirement, E is for estate, D is for debt, I is for investment, and T is for taxes. These are the basic components that you will need in the comprehensive financial plan that you will develop for your journey toward wealth accumulation and generational wealth.

Love always,
Dr. Deborah

About the Author

Dr. Deborah A. Niles, MD, FAAFP, is a board-certified family medicine physician and fellow of the American Academy of Family Physicians and a sought-after financial health expert, speaker, and media personality whose mission is to improve the financial health and well-being of communities. She has a bachelor of arts in neuroscience from the University of Pennsylvania and a medical degree from Drexel University. She completed her internship at Boston University Hospital and residency at the Department of Family Medicine and Community Health Robert Wood Johnson University Hospital. One of Dr. Deborah's proudest professional accomplishments is bringing the public's attention to secondhand smoke laws in Philadelphia.

Dr. Deborah is a member of the Delta Sigma Theta Sorority, Inc. Her hobbies include travel, photography, reading, writing, volunteering, speaking, and educating. She is the host of The *Ask Dr. Debby* show, where she covers health and wealth. Dr. Deborah lives in Plymouth Meeting, Pennsylvania.

Learn more at www.drdeborahniles.com

CREATING DISTINCTIVE BOOKS
WITH INTENTIONAL RESULTS

We're a collaborative group of creative masterminds
with a mission to produce high-quality books to position
you for monumental success in the marketplace.

Our professional team of writers, editors, designers,
and marketing strategists work closely together to ensure
that every detail of your book is a clear representation
of the message in your writing.

Want to know more?
Write to us at info@publishyourgift.com
or call (888) 949-6228

Discover great books, exclusive offers, and more at
www.PublishYourGift.com

Connect with us on social media

@publishyourgift

CPSIA information can be obtained
at www.ICGtesting.com
Printed in the USA
BVHW040946051121
620868BV00011B/235